River

MACMILLAN

Claire Llewellyn

Macmillan Education
Between Towns Road, Oxford OX4 3PP
A division of Macmillan Publishers Limited
Companies and representatives throughout the world

ISBN 978-0-230-43224-6 [International edition]
ISBN 978-0-230-43058-7 [Spanish edition]

Text written by Claire Llewellyn

The author has asserted her right to be identified as the author of this work in accordance with the Copyright, Design and Patents Act 1988.

First published 2013

Designed by Tim Mayer

Cover and title page photography reproduced with the kind permission of Shutterstock/repox (c), Shutterstock/Kjersti Joergensen (r)

The author and publishers would like to thank the following for permission to reproduce their photographic material:

Alamy/Ambient Images p29(t); The British Library Image Bank p18(b); Corbis/Michael DeYoung p3(cb); Corbis/Peter Johnson p3(ct); Corbis/Peter Johnson p11(t); Corbis/Michael DeYoung p26; Frank Lane Picture Agency/Do Van Dijck/Minden p7(t); FLPA/Dickie Duckett p3(b); FLPA/Dickie Duckett p29(b); Getty/Blend p18(t); Getty/Christophe Archambault/AFP p20; Getty/Daryl L. Hunter/Flickr p27(t); KF Archive pp6-7, 8-9, 14-15, 21(b), 23, 25(t, b); Shutterstock/Kjersti Joergensen p3(c); Shutterstock/Mayskyphoto pp4-5; Shutterstock/Evgeni Stefanov pp3(t), 5(t); Shutterstock/bumhills p5(b); Shutterstock/CAN BALCIOGLU p9(t); Shutterstock/repox p10; Shutterstock/B.S. Karan p11(b); Shutterstock/szefei p12; Shutterstock/Kang Khoon Seang p13(t); Shutterstock/Kjersti Joergensen p15(t); Shutterstock/Evgeny Dubinchuk p16; Sarah McClean p17; Shutterstock/Elena Elisseeva p19; Shutterstock/panda3800 p21(t); Shutterstock/Andy Z p22.; Shutterstock/Dan Breckwoldt p24; Shutterstock/mypokcik p27(b); Shutterstock/Dragana Gerasimoski p28.

These materials may contain links for third party websites. We have no control over, and are not responsible for, the contents of such third party websites. Please use care when accessing them.

Although we have tried to trace and contact copyright holders before publication, in some cases this has not been possible. If contacted, we will be pleased to rectify any errors or omissions at the earliest opportunity.

Printed and bound in China

International edition
2016 2015 2014 2013
10 9 8 7 6 5 4 3 2 1

Spanish edition
2016 2015 2014 2013
10 9 8 7 6 5 4 3 2 1

Contents

What is a river?

Rivers are bodies of mostly **fresh water** that flow to the sea. They can be very different from each other: some rivers flow quickly, others more slowly. Some rivers are narrow streams; others are so wide that you cannot see from one side to the other. A river may be all of these things at different places along its route or at different times of year.

Rivers are often beautiful. They are great for kayaking and other water sports.

Rivers are homes for
animals and plants.
They are important
to people, too. We travel on
them; we build towns on their
banks; we take fish from them
for food and we use their water
in many different ways.

Kingfishers build
their nests in river
banks and feed on
freshwater fish.

In this book you can find out about rivers:
how they change as they flow to the sea
and about their incredible power when
they flood the land.

Record-breaking rivers

The longest river in the world
is the River Nile in Africa. It
is 6,695 kilometres long and
flows through ten countries.
The shortest river is the
D river, in Oregon, USA. It is
just 37 metres long – the length of seven canoes.

The river's course

The place where a river begins is called its source. From there, the river flows downhill on its journey to the sea. The whole journey from start to finish is called the river's course.

Rivers start in different ways. This one is starting high in the mountains. This part of the river is called its source.

The river moves fast as it flows downhill.

The river gets bigger as other rivers and streams join it.

The river's mouth

Rivers carry a lot of mud, which sinks down around the mouth of the river. The mud makes a great feeding ground for birds. They push their beaks into the mud and pull out snails, worms and other juicy creatures.

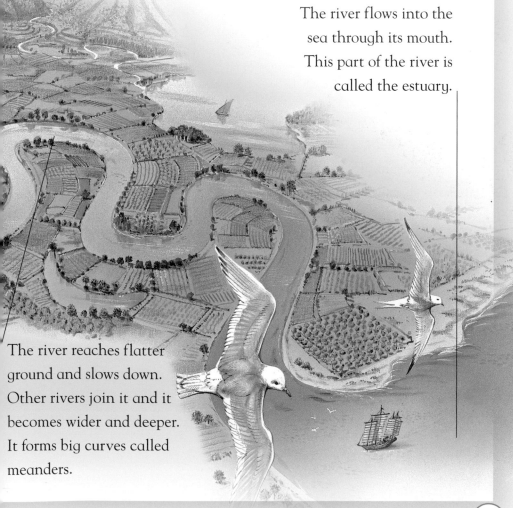

The river flows into the sea through its mouth. This part of the river is called the estuary.

The river reaches flatter ground and slows down. Other rivers join it and it becomes wider and deeper. It forms big curves called meanders.

The water cycle

The water on our planet is constantly moving between the sea, the air and the land. This movement is called the water cycle and rivers are an important part of it.

2. Water vapour rises up into the sky, where the air is colder.

1. The water cycle starts with the Sun. Its heat changes water on the surface of the land and sea into a gas, called water vapour.

Recycled water

The water cycle **recycles** the same water around our planet year after year, for billions of years. So the water you drink today probably flowed **downstream** past dinosaurs billions of years ago!

3. The vapour turns into droplets of water, which form clouds.

4. The droplets in the cloud join together and fall as rain.

5. The rain runs into rivers. They carry the water back to the sea, where the cycle starts again.

Shaping the land

Rivers follow the shape of the land but they can also change it. Moving water is very powerful. As a river flows over the land, it picks up stones and large rocks. These rocks roll along with the water. They carve the riverbed and chip at the banks, and make the river deeper and wider. This carving and chipping is called erosion.

This river in New Zealand is flowing so rapidly it can move huge rocks.

Victoria Falls,
in Africa

Sometimes a river flows over a cliff that it cannot erode. The water flows over the rock, and makes a waterfall.

On **limestone** hills, rainwater soaks down through the rock. The water drains into underground rivers, which erode the rocks to make tunnels and caves.

The Grand Canyon

Over 3–6 million years, the Colorado river in Arizona, USA, carved a deep **valley** out of solid rock. The valley, called the Grand Canyon, is 446 kilometres long and up to 29 kilometres wide.

River plants

Rivers make good **habitats** for plants because plants need water to grow. Trees that grow alongside rivers have long roots to grip the soil. This helps to hold the river bank together and stops it washing away.

Trees grow along a river in Malaysia.

Some plants grow mostly under the surface of the water, in places where the river flows very slowly. Others, such as reeds, have their roots under the water but their leaves grow up into the air above.

Giant water lilies have underwater roots. Their huge leaves float on the surface and are up to two metres wide!

Plants are important to the life of the river. Their leaves give off a gas called oxygen, which fish and other river life need to breathe. Plants also provide food for animals and safe places to nest or hide.

Spreading seeds

Many plants rely on rivers to spread their seeds. **Tropical** vines, called lianas, drop their seeds into rivers. The seeds float **downstream** to the sea and often grow on distant shores.

Reeds make perfect nests for water birds.

Animals of the river

Rivers are good habitats for animals. They are home to ducks and many kinds of fish, reptiles, and amphibians such as frogs and newts. In tropical countries, where the climate is warm, there are reptiles such as terrapins and turtles, crocodiles and snakes.

Smaller creatures, such as snails, shrimps, beetles and worms, also live in the river. Some insects, such as dragonflies, live in the water for the first stage of their life. Later, they

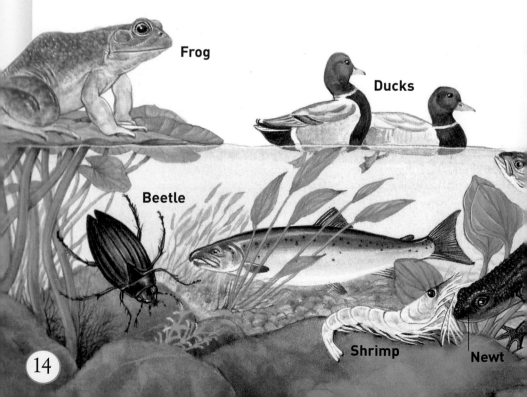

Frog

Ducks

Beetle

Shrimp

Newt

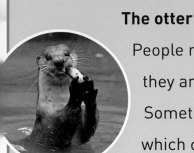

The otter

People rarely see otters because they are shy and **nocturnal** animals. Sometimes you find their droppings, which contain fish bones and scales and have a very fishy smell.

change into adults, and leave the water for a life in the air.

The river bank is home to mammals and birds. Water voles nest in holes in the banks. Water birds look for plants and worms, while otters and kingfishers hunt for fish.

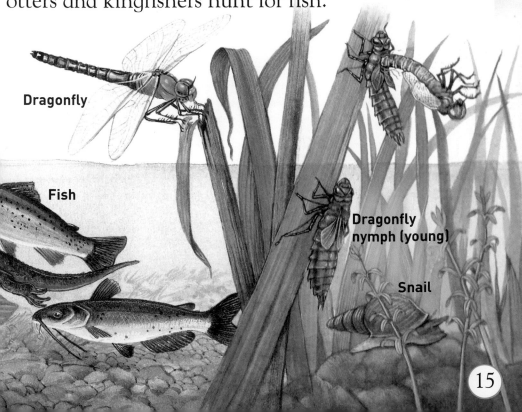

Dragonfly

Fish

Dragonfly nymph (young)

Snail

Rivers and people

People have always lived next to rivers. Many of the world's oldest and most important cities are on river banks. Cairo is on the Nile; Rome is on the Tiber and London is on the Thames.

Riverside towns and cities have lots of bridges so that people can cross the water. In New York City, USA, the Brooklyn Bridge links the city to the town of Brooklyn, on the other side of the East river. This has helped the city to grow.

Thousands of people who live in Brooklyn cross the bridge every day to work in New York's city centre.

Hundreds of people bathe in the River Ganges at
Varanasi, India. This town is an important place for Hindus.

Some rivers have a special meaning for
people. The Ganges river in India is **sacred** to
Hindus, who believe it washes away their sins.
During certain festivals, millions of **pilgrims**
travel to the Ganges to bathe in the water.

Using river water

We use the water from rivers in many different ways. In our homes we use it for drinking, washing, flushing the toilet and watering plants.

Watermills

People first built watermills on river banks about two thousand years ago. The rivers turned the waterwheels. The waterwheels turned heavy stones, which ground grain into flour. This painting shows a watermill over 600 years ago.

Factories use huge amounts of water. They use it to make things, and to cool down machinery when it gets too hot. Farmers use water, too. They take it directly from rivers to give to their animals and to **irrigate** their **crops**.

This big machine is irrigating the crops all around it.

The demand for water is growing and rivers are in danger. If we take too much water from them, river habitats begin to decline and fewer animals live in them. This affects both animals and people, who rely on rivers for food.

Rivers and floods

When a river is very full, it overflows and floods the land. This happens when snow suddenly melts, or heavy rain falls quickly. The river cannot hold all the water, so it bursts its banks.

Sudden floods are dangerous. They destroy buildings and crops, and people and animals may drown. In many parts of the world people try to prevent flood damage. They build barriers such as **dams** and **dykes**, which hold back the water.

In 2011, heavy rains in Thailand caused dangerous floods. Thousands of people had to leave their homes.

These farmers in Thailand are planting rice in flooded fields.

Some rivers flood every year and this can be useful for farmers. In India, China, Thailand and many other countries, rice farmers rely on rivers to flood their rice crops. The water keeps the rice plants cool, and controls weeds and pests.

River Nile

In ancient Egypt, the River Nile flooded every year. This was very important because the water and the **fertile** mud helped crops to grow. Good **harvests** helped Egypt and its people to become wealthy.

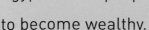

Dams and water power

Rivers flow at different rates throughout the year. In wet seasons, they get so full that sometimes they burst their banks. In dry seasons, they may dry up and disappear altogether. Dams control the flow of water.

A dam is a huge and very strong wall that crosses the width of a river. It stops the water flowing forwards. A big lake called a **reservoir** collects behind the dam. This stores fresh water for people to use in their homes.

The Hoover Dam is on the Colorado river in the USA.

A cruise ship
on the Yangtze
river in China
waits for
passengers.

Riverboats come in many shapes and sizes.
Small ferries carry people across the river. In
cities, pleasure boats take tourists to see the
sights. Giant cruisers are like hotels: they
carry people along the river for a few days at
a time.

River explorers

About 200 years ago, two
explorers, called Lewis and
Clark, travelled over 12,500
kilometres across America.
They travelled overland and
along many rivers to the
Pacific coast. Their discoveries
tempted people to move home
and farm the land.

Enjoying the river

Many rivers are beautiful places where people can relax and have fun. In places where the water flows slowly, people enjoy swimming or boating. In places where the river flows swiftly, kayaking is an exciting river sport.

On warm days, a river's leafy banks are a good place for a walk or a picnic.

Many people enjoy fishing in rivers. Trout and salmon are delicious to eat, but many people catch fish for sport, not food. If they catch a fish, they quickly free the hook and return the fish to the water.

Dragon boat races

Many boat races take place on rivers. Dragon-boat racing started in China but it is now popular all over the world. Each boat contains up to 20 pairs of rowers and a drummer. The rowers have to pull the oars in time with the beating drum.

27

Adding dirty water to rivers harms plant and animal life.

Looking after rivers

Pollution is a problem in many of our rivers. Factories pour their waste into them or pump warm water into them after using it to cool machines. Th waste contains harmful chemicals and the warm water is low in oxygen. Both can harm river life.

How to help rivers

- Save water whenever you can: turn off the tap when you brush your teeth; collect rainwater to water plants instead of tap water.

- Join a wildlife group. Local groups visit rivers and report pollution.

- Don't drop litter. Litter blows about in the wind and often ends up in rivers.

River clean-ups

Every year in the USA there is a national river clean-up. All over the country, thousands of people, including children, help to clean up local rivers and streams. The clean-ups began over 20 years ago. Every year, volunteers remove about one million kilos of rubbish from the rivers.

Farmers also pollute rivers. The **fertilizers** they use on crops, wash into rivers when it rains. This causes water plants to grow very fast. The plants upset the balance of the river and stop sunlight from entering the water.

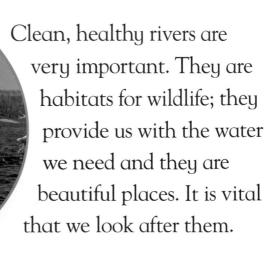

Clean, healthy rivers are very important. They are habitats for wildlife; they provide us with the water we need and they are beautiful places. It is vital that we look after them.

Glossary

banks the sides of a river

crops farmers grow these plants for food

dams walls across rivers which hold back the water

downstream the direction that a river flows, towards the sea

dykes ditches that hold back water

fertile fertile land is where plants grow well

fertilizers chemicals that we add to soil to make it more fertile

fresh water water in rivers, lakes and ice that is not salty like the sea

generators machines that make electricity

habitats the places where particular animals and plants live

harvests collections of crops that we grow and pick

Hindus followers of the Hindu religion

irrigate to water the land

limestone a soft type of rock

nocturnal awake and active at night

pilgrims people on a journey to a sacred place

pollution harmful waste that damages or poisons the environment

ports towns or cities with a harbour that boats use for loading and unloading goods

recycle to use again or make into something new

reservoir a lake holding water for use by people

sacred special or holy to people of a particular religion

tropical belonging to the tropics – warm, wet areas of the world

valley an area of low land between hills or mountains

31

Index